ALL ROADS

THAT LEAD TO

SUCCESS

HAVE TO PASS THROUGH

HARD WORK

Name: _____

Address: _____

Phone: _____

Email: _____

Business Overview

BUSINESS NAME:	
TAGLINE:	
WEBSITE:	

SOCIAL MEDIA HANDLES

MISSION STATEMENT

WHAT WILL SET YOU APART FROM YOUR COMPETITION?

TARGET CUSTOMER

CORE BIZ VALUES

BUSINESS GOALS

Business Brainstorm

I AM INSPIRED BY

WHY I WANT TO START THIS BUSINESS

WHO I WANT TO HELP

WHAT MAKES YOU UNIQUE? WHAT CAN YOU UNIQUELY OFFER TO YOUR CUSTOMER?

DEFINE YOUR PERFECT CUSTOMERS

GENDER:

SINGLE/ MARRIED:

AGE RANGE:

DO THEY HAVE KIDS?

HOW MUCH MONEY DO THEY MAKE?

WHAT DO THEY DO?

WHAT MOTIVATES THEM?

Goal Worksheet

LONG TERM BUSINESS GOAL

1 YEAR GOAL

WHY IS THIS GOAL IMPORTANT TO ME?

HOW WILL MY LIFE CHANGE

ROUTINES THAT WILL HELP ACHIEVE GOAL:

ACTION STEPS/ HABITS	J	F	M	A	M	J	J	A	S	O	N	D

Goal Timeline

WHEN	GOALS	ACTION STEPS
6 MONTHS		
1 YEARS		
2 YEARS		
3 YEARS		
4 YEARS		

Goal Breakdown

GOAL	STEPS/ HOW AM I GOING TO GET THERE	DUE DATE	X

GOAL	STEPS/ HOW AM I GOING TO GET THERE	DUE DATE	X

Annual Overview

JANUARY	FEBRUARY	MARCH

APRIL	MAY	JUNE

JULY	AUGUST	SEPTEMBER

OCTOBER	NOVEMBER	DECEMBER

Vendor Contact List

NAME:		COMPANY	
EMAIL:		PHONE	
ADDRESS:			
NOTES:			

NAME:		COMPANY	
EMAIL:		PHONE	
ADDRESS:			
NOTES:			

NAME:		COMPANY	
EMAIL:		PHONE	
ADDRESS:			
NOTES:			

NAME:		COMPANY	
EMAIL:		PHONE	
ADDRESS:			
NOTES:			

NAME:		COMPANY	
EMAIL:		PHONE	
ADDRESS:			
NOTES:			

NAME:		COMPANY	
EMAIL:		PHONE	
ADDRESS:			
NOTES:			

Vendor Contact List

NAME:		COMPANY	
EMAIL:		PHONE	
ADDRESS:			
NOTES:			

NAME:		COMPANY	
EMAIL:		PHONE	
ADDRESS:			
NOTES:			

NAME:		COMPANY	
EMAIL:		PHONE	
ADDRESS:			
NOTES:			

NAME:		COMPANY	
EMAIL:		PHONE	
ADDRESS:			
NOTES:			

NAME:		COMPANY	
EMAIL:		PHONE	
ADDRESS:			
NOTES:			

NAME:		COMPANY	
EMAIL:		PHONE	
ADDRESS:			
NOTES:			

Supplier Contact List

NAME:	
EMAIL:	
ADDRESS:	
NOTES:	

COMPANY	
PHONE	

NAME:	
EMAIL:	
ADDRESS:	
NOTES:	

COMPANY	
PHONE	

NAME:	
EMAIL:	
ADDRESS:	
NOTES:	

COMPANY	
PHONE	

NAME:	
EMAIL:	
ADDRESS:	
NOTES:	

COMPANY	
PHONE	

NAME:	
EMAIL:	
ADDRESS:	
NOTES:	

COMPANY	
PHONE	

NAME:	
EMAIL:	
ADDRESS:	
NOTES:	

COMPANY	
PHONE	

Supplier Contact List

NAME:		COMPANY	
EMAIL:		PHONE	
ADDRESS:			
NOTES:			

NAME:		COMPANY	
EMAIL:		PHONE	
ADDRESS:			
NOTES:			

NAME:		COMPANY	
EMAIL:		PHONE	
ADDRESS:			
NOTES:			

NAME:		COMPANY	
EMAIL:		PHONE	
ADDRESS:			
NOTES:			

NAME:		COMPANY	
EMAIL:		PHONE	
ADDRESS:			
NOTES:			

NAME:		COMPANY	
EMAIL:		PHONE	
ADDRESS:			
NOTES:			

Supply Inventory Log

DATE	ITEM	QTY	PRICE	SUPPLIER

Supply Inventory Log

DATE	ITEM	QTY	PRICE	SUPPLIER

Supply Inventory Log

DATE	ITEM	QTY	PRICE	SUPPLIER

Product Inventory Log

date	item	cost	# in stock	stocked	running low

Product Inventory Log

date	item	cost	# in stock	stocked	running low

Product Inventory Log

date	item	cost	# in stock	stocked	running low

DATE			**ORDER**	
RETURN CUSTOMER	YES	NO	....	

CUSTOMER DETAILS

NAME		SHIPPING ADRESS		
TEL				
EMAIL				
COMPANY		DATE SHIPPED		TRACKING No.
SHIPPING METHOD				

ITEM NO.	ITEM DESCRIPTION	QTY.	PRICE	DISCOUNT	TAX	TOTAL PRICE

COMFIRMATON

TOTAL UNIT PRICE		ADVANCED PAID		PAYMENT METHOD	
TOTAL DISCOUNT		REMAINING PAID		DATE PAID	
TOTAL TAX		TOTAL QUANTITY		**FINAL PRICE**	
NOTES:					

DATE			ORDER
RETURN CUSTOMER	YES	NO	

CUSTOMER DETAILS

NAME		SHIPPING ADRESS	
TEL			
EMAIL			
COMPANY		DATE SHIPPED	TRACKING No.
SHIPPING METHOD			

ITEM NO.	ITEM DESCRIPTION	QTY.	PRICE	DISCOUNT	TAX	TOTAL PRICE

COMFIRMATON

TOTAL UNIT PRICE		ADVANCED PAID		PAYMENT METHOD	
TOTAL DISCOUNT		REMAINING PAID		DATE PAID	
TOTAL TAX		TOTAL QUANTITY		FINAL PRICE	
NOTES:					

DATE			ORDER	
RETURN CUSTOMER	YES	NO		

CUSTOMER DETAILS

NAME		SHIPPING ADRESS		
TEL				
EMAIL				
COMPANY		DATE SHIPPED		TRACKING No.
SHIPPING METHOD				

ITEM NO.	ITEM DESCRIPTION	QTY.	PRICE	DISCOUNT	TAX	TOTAL PRICE

COMFIRMATON

TOTAL UNIT PRICE		ADVANCED PAID		PAYMENT METHOD	
TOTAL DISCOUNT		REMAINING PAID		DATE PAID	
TOTAL TAX		TOTAL QUANTITY		FINAL PRICE	

NOTES:

DATE				**ORDER**
RETURN CUSTOMER		YES	NO	....

CUSTOMER DETAILS

NAME		SHIPPING ADRESS	
TEL			
EMAIL			
COMPANY		DATE SHIPPED	TRACKING No.
SHIPPING METHOD			

ITEM NO.	ITEM DESCRIPTION	QTY.	PRICE	DISCOUNT	TAX	TOTAL PRICE

COMFIRMATON

TOTAL UNIT PRICE		ADVANCED PAID		PAYMENT METHOD	
TOTAL DISCOUNT		REMAINING PAID		DATE PAID	
TOTAL TAX		TOTAL QUANTITY		**FINAL PRICE**	
NOTES:					

DATE		**ORDER**	
RETURN CUSTOMER	YES	NO	....

CUSTOMER DETAILS

NAME		SHIPPING ADRESS	
TEL			
EMAIL			
COMPANY		DATE SHIPPED	TRACKING No.
SHIPPING METHOD			

ITEM NO.	ITEM DESCRIPTION	QTY.	PRICE	DISCOUNT	TAX	TOTAL PRICE

COMFIRMATON

TOTAL UNIT PRICE		ADVANCED PAID		PAYMENT METHOD	
TOTAL DISCOUNT		REMAINING PAID		DATE PAID	
TOTAL TAX		TOTAL QUANTITY		**FINAL PRICE**	
NOTES:					

DATE			**ORDER**	
RETURN CUSTOMER	YES	NO	....	

CUSTOMER DETAILS

NAME		SHIPPING ADRESS		
TEL				
EMAIL				
COMPANY		DATE SHIPPED		TRACKING No.
SHIPPING METHOD				

ITEM NO.	ITEM DESCRIPTION	QTY.	PRICE	DISCOUNT	TAX	TOTAL PRICE

COMFIRMATON

TOTAL UNIT PRICE		ADVANCED PAID		PAYMENT METHOD	
TOTAL DISCOUNT		REMAINING PAID		DATE PAID	
TOTAL TAX		TOTAL QUANTITY		FINAL PRICE	
NOTES:					

DATE			**ORDER**
RETURN CUSTOMER	YES	NO	

CUSTOMER DETAILS

NAME		SHIPPING ADRESS	
TEL			
EMAIL			
COMPANY		DATE SHIPPED	TRACKING No.
SHIPPING METHOD			

ITEM NO.	ITEM DESCRIPTION	QTY.	PRICE	DISCOUNT	TAX	TOTAL PRICE

COMFIRMATON

TOTAL UNIT PRICE		ADVANCED PAID		PAYMENT METHOD	
TOTAL DISCOUNT		REMAINING PAID		DATE PAID	
TOTAL TAX		TOTAL QUANTITY		**FINAL PRICE**	

NOTES:	

DATE			**ORDER**
RETURN CUSTOMER	YES	NO	....

CUSTOMER DETAILS

NAME		SHIPPING ADRESS	
TEL			
EMAIL			
COMPANY		DATE SHIPPED	TRACKING No.
SHIPPING METHOD			

ITEM NO.	ITEM DESCRIPTION	QTY.	PRICE	DISCOUNT	TAX	TOTAL PRICE

COMFIRMATON

TOTAL UNIT PRICE		ADVANCED PAID		PAYMENT METHOD	
TOTAL DISCOUNT		REMAINING PAID		DATE PAID	
TOTAL TAX		TOTAL QUANTITY		**FINAL PRICE**	
NOTES:					

DATE		ORDER	
RETURN CUSTOMER	YES	NO	....

CUSTOMER DETAILS

NAME		SHIPPING ADRESS	
TEL			
EMAIL			
COMPANY		DATE SHIPPED	TRACKING No.
SHIPPING METHOD			

ITEM NO.	ITEM DESCRIPTION	QTY.	PRICE	DISCOUNT	TAX	TOTAL PRICE

COMFIRMATON

TOTAL UNIT PRICE		ADVANCED PAID		PAYMENT METHOD	
TOTAL DISCOUNT		REMAINING PAID		DATE PAID	
TOTAL TAX		TOTAL QUANTITY		FINAL PRICE	
NOTES:					

DATE				ORDER	
RETURN CUSTOMER	YES		NO	....	

CUSTOMER DETAILS

NAME		SHIPPING ADRESS	
TEL			
EMAIL			
COMPANY		DATE SHIPPED	TRACKING No.
SHIPPING METHOD			

ITEM NO.	ITEM DESCRIPTION	QTY.	PRICE	DISCOUNT	TAX	TOTAL PRICE

COMFIRMATON

TOTAL UNIT PRICE		ADVANCED PAID		PAYMENT METHOD	
TOTAL DISCOUNT		REMAINING PAID		DATE PAID	
TOTAL TAX		TOTAL QUANTITY		FINAL PRICE	

NOTES:

DATE			ORDER		
RETURN CUSTOMER	YES	NO	....		

CUSTOMER DETAILS

NAME		SHIPPING ADRESS		
TEL				
EMAIL				
COMPANY		DATE SHIPPED	TRACKING No.	
SHIPPING METHOD				

ITEM NO.	ITEM DESCRIPTION	QTY.	PRICE	DISCOUNT	TAX	TOTAL PRICE

COMFIRMATON

TOTAL UNIT PRICE		ADVANCED PAID		PAYMENT METHOD	
TOTAL DISCOUNT		REMAINING PAID		DATE PAID	
TOTAL TAX		TOTAL QUANTITY		FINAL PRICE	

NOTES:

DATE			ORDER
RETURN CUSTOMER	YES	NO	....

CUSTOMER DETAILS

NAME		SHIPPING ADRESS	
TEL			
EMAIL			
COMPANY		DATE SHIPPED	TRACKING No.
SHIPPING METHOD			

ITEM NO.	ITEM DESCRIPTION	QTY.	PRICE	DISCOUNT	TAX	TOTAL PRICE

COMFIRMATON

TOTAL UNIT PRICE		ADVANCED PAID		PAYMENT METHOD	
TOTAL DISCOUNT		REMAINING PAID		DATE PAID	
TOTAL TAX		TOTAL QUANTITY		FINAL PRICE	

NOTES:

DATE		**ORDER**	
RETURN CUSTOMER	YES	NO	

CUSTOMER DETAILS

NAME		SHIPPING ADRESS	
TEL			
EMAIL			
COMPANY		DATE SHIPPED	TRACKING No.
SHIPPING METHOD			

ITEM NO.	ITEM DESCRIPTION	QTY.	PRICE	DISCOUNT	TAX	TOTAL PRICE

COMFIRMATON

TOTAL UNIT PRICE		ADVANCED PAID		PAYMENT METHOD	
TOTAL DISCOUNT		REMAINING PAID		DATE PAID	
TOTAL TAX		TOTAL QUANTITY		**FINAL PRICE**	
NOTES:					

DATE			**ORDER**
RETURN CUSTOMER	YES	NO	

CUSTOMER DETAILS

NAME		SHIPPING ADRESS	
TEL			
EMAIL			
COMPANY		DATE SHIPPED	TRACKING No.
SHIPPING METHOD			

ITEM NO.	ITEM DESCRIPTION	QTY.	PRICE	DISCOUNT	TAX	TOTAL PRICE

COMFIRMATON

TOTAL UNIT PRICE		ADVANCED PAID		PAYMENT METHOD	
TOTAL DISCOUNT		REMAINING PAID		DATE PAID	
TOTAL TAX		TOTAL QUANTITY		**FINAL PRICE**	

NOTES:	

DATE		**ORDER**	
RETURN CUSTOMER	YES	NO	....

CUSTOMER DETAILS

NAME		SHIPPING ADRESS	
TEL			
EMAIL			
COMPANY		DATE SHIPPED	TRACKING No.
SHIPPING METHOD			

ITEM NO.	ITEM DESCRIPTION	QTY.	PRICE	DISCOUNT	TAX	TOTAL PRICE

COMFIRMATON

TOTAL UNIT PRICE		ADVANCED PAID		PAYMENT METHOD	
TOTAL DISCOUNT		REMAINING PAID		DATE PAID	
TOTAL TAX		TOTAL QUANTITY		FINAL PRICE	
NOTES:					

DATE		**ORDER**	
RETURN CUSTOMER	YES	NO	

CUSTOMER DETAILS

NAME		SHIPPING ADRESS	
TEL			
EMAIL			
COMPANY		DATE SHIPPED	TRACKING No.
SHIPPING METHOD			

ITEM NO.	ITEM DESCRIPTION	QTY.	PRICE	DISCOUNT	TAX	TOTAL PRICE

COMFIRMATON

TOTAL UNIT PRICE		ADVANCED PAID		PAYMENT METHOD	
TOTAL DISCOUNT		REMAINING PAID		DATE PAID	
TOTAL TAX		TOTAL QUANTITY		**FINAL PRICE**	
NOTES:					

DATE		**ORDER**	
RETURN CUSTOMER	YES	NO	....

CUSTOMER DETAILS

NAME		SHIPPING ADRESS	
TEL			
EMAIL			
COMPANY		DATE SHIPPED	TRACKING No.
SHIPPING METHOD			

ITEM NO.	ITEM DESCRIPTION	QTY.	PRICE	DISCOUNT	TAX	TOTAL PRICE

COMFIRMATON

TOTAL UNIT PRICE		ADVANCED PAID		PAYMENT METHOD	
TOTAL DISCOUNT		REMAINING PAID		DATE PAID	
TOTAL TAX		TOTAL QUANTITY		**FINAL PRICE**	
NOTES:					

DATE			**ORDER**	
RETURN CUSTOMER	YES	NO	....	

CUSTOMER DETAILS

NAME		SHIPPING ADRESS	
TEL			
EMAIL			
COMPANY		DATE SHIPPED	TRACKING No.
SHIPPING METHOD			

ITEM NO.	ITEM DESCRIPTION	QTY.	PRICE	DISCOUNT	TAX	TOTAL PRICE

COMFIRMATON

TOTAL UNIT PRICE		ADVANCED PAID		PAYMENT METHOD	
TOTAL DISCOUNT		REMAINING PAID		DATE PAID	
TOTAL TAX		TOTAL QUANTITY		FINAL PRICE	
NOTES:					

DATE		**ORDER**	
RETURN CUSTOMER	YES	NO	

CUSTOMER DETAILS

NAME		SHIPPING ADRESS	
TEL			
EMAIL			
COMPANY		DATE SHIPPED	TRACKING No.
SHIPPING METHOD			

ITEM NO.	ITEM DESCRIPTION	QTY.	PRICE	DISCOUNT	TAX	TOTAL PRICE

COMFIRMATON

TOTAL UNIT PRICE		ADVANCED PAID		PAYMENT METHOD	
TOTAL DISCOUNT		REMAINING PAID		DATE PAID	
TOTAL TAX		TOTAL QUANTITY		**FINAL PRICE**	
NOTES:					

DATE			ORDER	
RETURN CUSTOMER	YES	NO	....	

CUSTOMER DETAILS

NAME		SHIPPING ADRESS	
TEL			
EMAIL			
COMPANY		DATE SHIPPED	TRACKING No.
SHIPPING METHOD			

ITEM NO.	ITEM DESCRIPTION	QTY.	PRICE	DISCOUNT	TAX	TOTAL PRICE

COMFIRMATON

TOTAL UNIT PRICE		ADVANCED PAID		PAYMENT METHOD	
TOTAL DISCOUNT		REMAINING PAID		DATE PAID	
TOTAL TAX		TOTAL QUANTITY		FINAL PRICE	
NOTES:					

DATE			ORDER
RETURN CUSTOMER	YES	NO	....

CUSTOMER DETAILS

NAME		SHIPPING ADRESS	
TEL			
EMAIL			
COMPANY		DATE SHIPPED	TRACKING No.
SHIPPING METHOD			

ITEM NO.	ITEM DESCRIPTION	QTY.	PRICE	DISCOUNT	TAX	TOTAL PRICE

COMFIRMATON

TOTAL UNIT PRICE		ADVANCED PAID		PAYMENT METHOD	
TOTAL DISCOUNT		REMAINING PAID		DATE PAID	
TOTAL TAX		TOTAL QUANTITY		FINAL PRICE	
NOTES:					

DATE			ORDER
RETURN CUSTOMER	YES	NO	....

CUSTOMER DETAILS

NAME		SHIPPING ADRESS	
TEL			
EMAIL			
COMPANY		DATE SHIPPED	TRACKING No.
SHIPPING METHOD			

ITEM NO.	ITEM DESCRIPTION	QTY.	PRICE	DISCOUNT	TAX	TOTAL PRICE

COMFIRMATON

TOTAL UNIT PRICE		ADVANCED PAID		PAYMENT METHOD	
TOTAL DISCOUNT		REMAINING PAID		DATE PAID	
TOTAL TAX		TOTAL QUANTITY		FINAL PRICE	
NOTES:					

DATE		ORDER	
RETURN CUSTOMER	YES	NO	

CUSTOMER DETAILS

NAME		SHIPPING ADRESS	
TEL			
EMAIL			
COMPANY		DATE SHIPPED	TRACKING No.
SHIPPING METHOD			

ITEM NO.	ITEM DESCRIPTION	QTY.	PRICE	DISCOUNT	TAX	TOTAL PRICE

COMFIRMATON

TOTAL UNIT PRICE		ADVANCED PAID		PAYMENT METHOD	
TOTAL DISCOUNT		REMAINING PAID		DATE PAID	
TOTAL TAX		TOTAL QUANTITY		FINAL PRICE	
NOTES:					

DATE			ORDER
RETURN CUSTOMER	YES	NO	....

CUSTOMER DETAILS

NAME		SHIPPING ADRESS	
TEL			
EMAIL			
COMPANY		DATE SHIPPED	TRACKING No.
SHIPPING METHOD			

ITEM NO.	ITEM DESCRIPTION	QTY.	PRICE	DISCOUNT	TAX	TOTAL PRICE

COMFIRMATON

TOTAL UNIT PRICE		ADVANCED PAID		PAYMENT METHOD	
TOTAL DISCOUNT		REMAINING PAID		DATE PAID	
TOTAL TAX		TOTAL QUANTITY		FINAL PRICE	
NOTES:					

DATE		ORDER	
RETURN CUSTOMER	YES	NO	....

CUSTOMER DETAILS

NAME		SHIPPING ADRESS	
TEL			
EMAIL			
COMPANY		DATE SHIPPED	TRACKING No.
SHIPPING METHOD			

ITEM NO.	ITEM DESCRIPTION	QTY.	PRICE	DISCOUNT	TAX	TOTAL PRICE

COMFIRMATON

TOTAL UNIT PRICE		ADVANCED PAID		PAYMENT METHOD	
TOTAL DISCOUNT		REMAINING PAID		DATE PAID	
TOTAL TAX		TOTAL QUANTITY		FINAL PRICE	

NOTES:

DATE			**ORDER**
RETURN CUSTOMER	YES	NO	....

CUSTOMER DETAILS

NAME		SHIPPING ADRESS	
TEL			
EMAIL			
COMPANY		DATE SHIPPED	TRACKING No.
SHIPPING METHOD			

ITEM NO.	ITEM DESCRIPTION	QTY.	PRICE	DISCOUNT	TAX	TOTAL PRICE

COMFIRMATON

TOTAL UNIT PRICE		ADVANCED PAID		PAYMENT METHOD	
TOTAL DISCOUNT		REMAINING PAID		DATE PAID	
TOTAL TAX		TOTAL QUANTITY		**FINAL PRICE**	

NOTES:	

DATE		ORDER	
RETURN CUSTOMER	YES	NO	

CUSTOMER DETAILS

NAME		SHIPPING ADRESS	
TEL			
EMAIL			
COMPANY		DATE SHIPPED	TRACKING No.
SHIPPING METHOD			

ITEM NO.	ITEM DESCRIPTION	QTY.	PRICE	DISCOUNT	TAX	TOTAL PRICE

COMFIRMATON

TOTAL UNIT PRICE		ADVANCED PAID		PAYMENT METHOD	
TOTAL DISCOUNT		REMAINING PAID		DATE PAID	
TOTAL TAX		TOTAL QUANTITY		FINAL PRICE	

NOTES:

DATE			**ORDER**
RETURN CUSTOMER	YES	NO	

CUSTOMER DETAILS

NAME		SHIPPING ADRESS	
TEL			
EMAIL			
COMPANY		DATE SHIPPED	TRACKING No.
SHIPPING METHOD			

ITEM NO.	ITEM DESCRIPTION	QTY.	PRICE	DISCOUNT	TAX	TOTAL PRICE

COMFIRMATON

TOTAL UNIT PRICE		ADVANCED PAID		PAYMENT METHOD	
TOTAL DISCOUNT		REMAINING PAID		DATE PAID	
TOTAL TAX		TOTAL QUANTITY		FINAL PRICE	
NOTES:					

DATE			**ORDER**	
RETURN CUSTOMER	YES	NO		

CUSTOMER DETAILS

NAME		SHIPPING ADRESS	
TEL			
EMAIL			
COMPANY		DATE SHIPPED	TRACKING No.
SHIPPING METHOD			

ITEM NO.	ITEM DESCRIPTION	QTY.	PRICE	DISCOUNT	TAX	TOTAL PRICE

COMFIRMATON

TOTAL UNIT PRICE		ADVANCED PAID		PAYMENT METHOD	
TOTAL DISCOUNT		REMAINING PAID		DATE PAID	
TOTAL TAX		TOTAL QUANTITY		**FINAL PRICE**	
NOTES:					

DATE				**ORDER**
RETURN CUSTOMER	YES		NO	

CUSTOMER DETAILS

NAME		SHIPPING ADRESS	
TEL			
EMAIL			
COMPANY		DATE SHIPPED	TRACKING No.
SHIPPING METHOD			

ITEM NO.	ITEM DESCRIPTION	QTY.	PRICE	DISCOUNT	TAX	TOTAL PRICE

COMFIRMATON

TOTAL UNIT PRICE		ADVANCED PAID		PAYMENT METHOD	
TOTAL DISCOUNT		REMAINING PAID		DATE PAID	
TOTAL TAX		TOTAL QUANTITY		**FINAL PRICE**	

NOTES:	

DATE			**ORDER**	
RETURN CUSTOMER	YES	NO	....	

CUSTOMER DETAILS

NAME		SHIPPING ADRESS		
TEL				
EMAIL				
COMPANY		DATE SHIPPED		TRACKING No.
SHIPPING METHOD				

ITEM NO.	ITEM DESCRIPTION	QTY.	PRICE	DISCOUNT	TAX	TOTAL PRICE

COMFIRMATON

TOTAL UNIT PRICE		ADVANCED PAID		PAYMENT METHOD	
TOTAL DISCOUNT		REMAINING PAID		DATE PAID	
TOTAL TAX		TOTAL QUANTITY		**FINAL PRICE**	
NOTES:					

DATE			**ORDER**
RETURN CUSTOMER	YES	NO	....

CUSTOMER DETAILS

NAME		SHIPPING ADRESS	
TEL			
EMAIL			
COMPANY		DATE SHIPPED	TRACKING No.
SHIPPING METHOD			

ITEM NO.	ITEM DESCRIPTION	QTY.	PRICE	DISCOUNT	TAX	TOTAL PRICE

COMFIRMATON

TOTAL UNIT PRICE		ADVANCED PAID		PAYMENT METHOD	
TOTAL DISCOUNT		REMAINING PAID		DATE PAID	
TOTAL TAX		TOTAL QUANTITY		FINAL PRICE	
NOTES:					

DATE			ORDER	
RETURN CUSTOMER	YES	NO	....	

CUSTOMER DETAILS

NAME		SHIPPING ADRESS	
TEL			
EMAIL			
COMPANY		DATE SHIPPED	TRACKING No.
SHIPPING METHOD			

ITEM NO.	ITEM DESCRIPTION	QTY.	PRICE	DISCOUNT	TAX	TOTAL PRICE

COMFIRMATON

TOTAL UNIT PRICE		ADVANCED PAID		PAYMENT METHOD	
TOTAL DISCOUNT		REMAINING PAID		DATE PAID	
TOTAL TAX		TOTAL QUANTITY		FINAL PRICE	
NOTES:					

DATE			**ORDER**	
RETURN CUSTOMER	YES	NO	....	

CUSTOMER DETAILS

NAME		SHIPPING ADRESS	
TEL			
EMAIL			
COMPANY		DATE SHIPPED	TRACKING No.
SHIPPING METHOD			

ITEM NO.	ITEM DESCRIPTION	QTY.	PRICE	DISCOUNT	TAX	TOTAL PRICE

COMFIRMATON

TOTAL UNIT PRICE		ADVANCED PAID		PAYMENT METHOD	
TOTAL DISCOUNT		REMAINING PAID		DATE PAID	
TOTAL TAX		TOTAL QUANTITY		FINAL PRICE	
NOTES:					

DATE			ORDER
RETURN CUSTOMER	YES	NO	....

CUSTOMER DETAILS

NAME		SHIPPING ADRESS	
TEL			
EMAIL			
COMPANY		DATE SHIPPED	TRACKING No.
SHIPPING METHOD			

ITEM NO.	ITEM DESCRIPTION	QTY.	PRICE	DISCOUNT	TAX	TOTAL PRICE

COMFIRMATON

TOTAL UNIT PRICE		ADVANCED PAID		PAYMENT METHOD	
TOTAL DISCOUNT		REMAINING PAID		DATE PAID	
TOTAL TAX		TOTAL QUANTITY		FINAL PRICE	

NOTES:

DATE			**ORDER**
RETURN CUSTOMER	YES	NO	

CUSTOMER DETAILS

NAME		SHIPPING ADRESS	
TEL			
EMAIL			
COMPANY		DATE SHIPPED	TRACKING No.
SHIPPING METHOD			

ITEM NO.	ITEM DESCRIPTION	QTY.	PRICE	DISCOUNT	TAX	TOTAL PRICE

COMFIRMATON

TOTAL UNIT PRICE		ADVANCED PAID		PAYMENT METHOD	
TOTAL DISCOUNT		REMAINING PAID		DATE PAID	
TOTAL TAX		TOTAL QUANTITY		FINAL PRICE	
NOTES:					

DATE				ORDER	
RETURN CUSTOMER		YES	NO		

CUSTOMER DETAILS

NAME		SHIPPING ADRESS	
TEL			
EMAIL			
COMPANY		DATE SHIPPED	TRACKING No.
SHIPPING METHOD			

ITEM NO.	ITEM DESCRIPTION	QTY.	PRICE	DISCOUNT	TAX	TOTAL PRICE

COMFIRMATON

TOTAL UNIT PRICE		ADVANCED PAID		PAYMENT METHOD	
TOTAL DISCOUNT		REMAINING PAID		DATE PAID	
TOTAL TAX		TOTAL QUANTITY		FINAL PRICE	
NOTES:					

DATE		ORDER		
RETURN CUSTOMER	YES	NO		

CUSTOMER DETAILS

NAME		SHIPPING ADRESS	
TEL			
EMAIL			
COMPANY		DATE SHIPPED	TRACKING No.
SHIPPING METHOD			

ITEM NO.	ITEM DESCRIPTION	QTY.	PRICE	DISCOUNT	TAX	TOTAL PRICE

COMFIRMATON

TOTAL UNIT PRICE		ADVANCED PAID		PAYMENT METHOD	
TOTAL DISCOUNT		REMAINING PAID		DATE PAID	
TOTAL TAX		TOTAL QUANTITY		FINAL PRICE	
NOTES:					

DATE		**ORDER**	
RETURN CUSTOMER	YES	NO	
		....	

CUSTOMER DETAILS

NAME		SHIPPING ADRESS	
TEL			
EMAIL			
COMPANY		DATE SHIPPED	TRACKING No.
SHIPPING METHOD			

ITEM NO.	ITEM DESCRIPTION	QTY.	PRICE	DISCOUNT	TAX	TOTAL PRICE

COMFIRMATON

TOTAL UNIT PRICE		ADVANCED PAID		PAYMENT METHOD	
TOTAL DISCOUNT		REMAINING PAID		DATE PAID	
TOTAL TAX		TOTAL QUANTITY		FINAL PRICE	
NOTES:					

DATE			**ORDER**
RETURN CUSTOMER	YES	NO	....

CUSTOMER DETAILS

NAME		SHIPPING ADRESS	
TEL			
EMAIL			
COMPANY		DATE SHIPPED	TRACKING No.
SHIPPING METHOD			

ITEM NO.	ITEM DESCRIPTION	QTY.	PRICE	DISCOUNT	TAX	TOTAL PRICE

COMFIRMATON

TOTAL UNIT PRICE		ADVANCED PAID		PAYMENT METHOD	
TOTAL DISCOUNT		REMAINING PAID		DATE PAID	
TOTAL TAX		TOTAL QUANTITY		FINAL PRICE	
NOTES:					

DATE			ORDER	
RETURN CUSTOMER	YES	NO	....	

CUSTOMER DETAILS

NAME		SHIPPING ADRESS		
TEL				
EMAIL				
COMPANY		DATE SHIPPED	TRACKING No.	
SHIPPING METHOD				

ITEM NO.	ITEM DESCRIPTION	QTY.	PRICE	DISCOUNT	TAX	TOTAL PRICE

COMFIRMATON

TOTAL UNIT PRICE		ADVANCED PAID		PAYMENT METHOD	
TOTAL DISCOUNT		REMAINING PAID		DATE PAID	
TOTAL TAX		TOTAL QUANTITY		FINAL PRICE	
NOTES:					

DATE			ORDER
RETURN CUSTOMER	YES	NO	

CUSTOMER DETAILS			
NAME		SHIPPING ADRESS	
TEL			
EMAIL			
COMPANY		DATE SHIPPED	TRACKING No.
SHIPPING METHOD			

ITEM NO.	ITEM DESCRIPTION	QTY.	PRICE	DISCOUNT	TAX	TOTAL PRICE

COMFIRMATON					
TOTAL UNIT PRICE		ADVANCED PAID		PAYMENT METHOD	
TOTAL DISCOUNT		REMAINING PAID		DATE PAID	
TOTAL TAX		TOTAL QUANTITY		FINAL PRICE	
NOTES:					

DATE		ORDER	
RETURN CUSTOMER	YES	NO	

CUSTOMER DETAILS

NAME		SHIPPING ADRESS	
TEL			
EMAIL			
COMPANY		DATE SHIPPED	TRACKING No.
SHIPPING METHOD			

ITEM NO.	ITEM DESCRIPTION	QTY.	PRICE	DISCOUNT	TAX	TOTAL PRICE

COMFIRMATON

TOTAL UNIT PRICE		ADVANCED PAID		PAYMENT METHOD	
TOTAL DISCOUNT		REMAINING PAID		DATE PAID	
TOTAL TAX		TOTAL QUANTITY		FINAL PRICE	

NOTES:

DATE		ORDER	
RETURN CUSTOMER	YES	NO	

CUSTOMER DETAILS

NAME		SHIPPING ADRESS	
TEL			
EMAIL			
COMPANY		DATE SHIPPED	TRACKING No.
SHIPPING METHOD			

ITEM NO.	ITEM DESCRIPTION	QTY.	PRICE	DISCOUNT	TAX	TOTAL PRICE

COMFIRMATON

TOTAL UNIT PRICE		ADVANCED PAID		PAYMENT METHOD	
TOTAL DISCOUNT		REMAINING PAID		DATE PAID	
TOTAL TAX		TOTAL QUANTITY		FINAL PRICE	
NOTES:					

DATE			**ORDER**	
RETURN CUSTOMER	YES	NO	....	

CUSTOMER DETAILS

NAME		SHIPPING ADRESS	
TEL			
EMAIL			
COMPANY		DATE SHIPPED	TRACKING No.
SHIPPING METHOD			

ITEM NO.	ITEM DESCRIPTION	QTY.	PRICE	DISCOUNT	TAX	TOTAL PRICE

COMFIRMATON

TOTAL UNIT PRICE		ADVANCED PAID		PAYMENT METHOD	
TOTAL DISCOUNT		REMAINING PAID		DATE PAID	
TOTAL TAX		TOTAL QUANTITY		**FINAL PRICE**	
NOTES:					

DATE		**ORDER**	
RETURN CUSTOMER	YES	NO	....

CUSTOMER DETAILS

NAME		SHIPPING ADRESS	
TEL			
EMAIL			
COMPANY		DATE SHIPPED	TRACKING No.
SHIPPING METHOD			

ITEM NO.	ITEM DESCRIPTION	QTY.	PRICE	DISCOUNT	TAX	TOTAL PRICE

COMFIRMATON

TOTAL UNIT PRICE		ADVANCED PAID		PAYMENT METHOD	
TOTAL DISCOUNT		REMAINING PAID		DATE PAID	
TOTAL TAX		TOTAL QUANTITY		**FINAL PRICE**	
NOTES:					

DATE		ORDER	
RETURN CUSTOMER	YES	NO	

CUSTOMER DETAILS

NAME		SHIPPING ADRESS	
TEL			
EMAIL			
COMPANY		DATE SHIPPED	TRACKING No.
SHIPPING METHOD			

ITEM NO.	ITEM DESCRIPTION	QTY.	PRICE	DISCOUNT	TAX	TOTAL PRICE

COMFIRMATON

TOTAL UNIT PRICE		ADVANCED PAID		PAYMENT METHOD	
TOTAL DISCOUNT		REMAINING PAID		DATE PAID	
TOTAL TAX		TOTAL QUANTITY		FINAL PRICE	
NOTES:					

DATE		**ORDER**	
RETURN CUSTOMER	YES	NO	....

CUSTOMER DETAILS

NAME		SHIPPING ADRESS	
TEL			
EMAIL			
COMPANY		DATE SHIPPED	TRACKING No.
SHIPPING METHOD			

ITEM NO.	ITEM DESCRIPTION	QTY.	PRICE	DISCOUNT	TAX	TOTAL PRICE

COMFIRMATON

TOTAL UNIT PRICE		ADVANCED PAID		PAYMENT METHOD	
TOTAL DISCOUNT		REMAINING PAID		DATE PAID	
TOTAL TAX		TOTAL QUANTITY		**FINAL PRICE**	
NOTES:					

DATE			ORDER	
RETURN CUSTOMER	YES	NO	....	

CUSTOMER DETAILS

NAME		SHIPPING ADRESS	
TEL			
EMAIL			
COMPANY		DATE SHIPPED	TRACKING No.
SHIPPING METHOD			

ITEM NO.	ITEM DESCRIPTION	QTY.	PRICE	DISCOUNT	TAX	TOTAL PRICE

COMFIRMATON

TOTAL UNIT PRICE		ADVANCED PAID		PAYMENT METHOD	
TOTAL DISCOUNT		REMAINING PAID		DATE PAID	
TOTAL TAX		TOTAL QUANTITY		FINAL PRICE	
NOTES:					

DATE			**ORDER**
RETURN CUSTOMER	YES	NO	

CUSTOMER DETAILS

NAME		SHIPPING ADRESS	
TEL			
EMAIL			
COMPANY		DATE SHIPPED	TRACKING No.
SHIPPING METHOD			

ITEM NO.	ITEM DESCRIPTION	QTY.	PRICE	DISCOUNT	TAX	TOTAL PRICE

COMFIRMATON

TOTAL UNIT PRICE		ADVANCED PAID		PAYMENT METHOD	
TOTAL DISCOUNT		REMAINING PAID		DATE PAID	
TOTAL TAX		TOTAL QUANTITY		FINAL PRICE	

NOTES:	

DATE			ORDER	
RETURN CUSTOMER	YES	NO		

CUSTOMER DETAILS

NAME		SHIPPING ADRESS		
TEL				
EMAIL				
COMPANY		DATE SHIPPED		TRACKING No.
SHIPPING METHOD				

ITEM NO.	ITEM DESCRIPTION	QTY.	PRICE	DISCOUNT	TAX	TOTAL PRICE

COMFIRMATON

TOTAL UNIT PRICE		ADVANCED PAID		PAYMENT METHOD	
TOTAL DISCOUNT		REMAINING PAID		DATE PAID	
TOTAL TAX		TOTAL QUANTITY		FINAL PRICE	
NOTES:					

DATE		**ORDER**	
RETURN CUSTOMER	YES	NO	

CUSTOMER DETAILS

NAME		SHIPPING ADRESS	
TEL			
EMAIL			
COMPANY		DATE SHIPPED	TRACKING No.
SHIPPING METHOD			

ITEM NO.	ITEM DESCRIPTION	QTY.	PRICE	DISCOUNT	TAX	TOTAL PRICE

COMFIRMATON

TOTAL UNIT PRICE		ADVANCED PAID		PAYMENT METHOD	
TOTAL DISCOUNT		REMAINING PAID		DATE PAID	
TOTAL TAX		TOTAL QUANTITY		FINAL PRICE	

NOTES:

DATE			**ORDER**	
RETURN CUSTOMER	YES	NO	....	

CUSTOMER DETAILS

NAME		SHIPPING ADRESS		
TEL				
EMAIL				
COMPANY		DATE SHIPPED		TRACKING No.
SHIPPING METHOD				

ITEM NO.	ITEM DESCRIPTION	QTY.	PRICE	DISCOUNT	TAX	TOTAL PRICE

COMFIRMATON

TOTAL UNIT PRICE		ADVANCED PAID		PAYMENT METHOD	
TOTAL DISCOUNT		REMAINING PAID		DATE PAID	
TOTAL TAX		TOTAL QUANTITY		**FINAL PRICE**	
NOTES:					

DATE			**ORDER**	
RETURN CUSTOMER	YES	NO	....	

CUSTOMER DETAILS

NAME		SHIPPING ADRESS	
TEL			
EMAIL			
COMPANY		DATE SHIPPED	TRACKING No.
SHIPPING METHOD			

ITEM NO.	ITEM DESCRIPTION	QTY.	PRICE	DISCOUNT	TAX	TOTAL PRICE

COMFIRMATON

TOTAL UNIT PRICE		ADVANCED PAID		PAYMENT METHOD	
TOTAL DISCOUNT		REMAINING PAID		DATE PAID	
TOTAL TAX		TOTAL QUANTITY		FINAL PRICE	
NOTES:					

DATE		ORDER	
RETURN CUSTOMER	YES	NO	

CUSTOMER DETAILS

NAME		SHIPPING ADRESS	
TEL			
EMAIL			
COMPANY		DATE SHIPPED	TRACKING No.
SHIPPING METHOD			

ITEM NO.	ITEM DESCRIPTION	QTY.	PRICE	DISCOUNT	TAX	TOTAL PRICE

COMFIRMATON

TOTAL UNIT PRICE		ADVANCED PAID		PAYMENT METHOD	
TOTAL DISCOUNT		REMAINING PAID		DATE PAID	
TOTAL TAX		TOTAL QUANTITY		FINAL PRICE	
NOTES:					

DATE		ORDER	
RETURN CUSTOMER	YES	NO	....

CUSTOMER DETAILS

NAME		SHIPPING ADRESS	
TEL			
EMAIL			
COMPANY		DATE SHIPPED	TRACKING No.
SHIPPING METHOD			

ITEM NO.	ITEM DESCRIPTION	QTY.	PRICE	DISCOUNT	TAX	TOTAL PRICE

COMFIRMATON

TOTAL UNIT PRICE		ADVANCED PAID		PAYMENT METHOD	
TOTAL DISCOUNT		REMAINING PAID		DATE PAID	
TOTAL TAX		TOTAL QUANTITY		FINAL PRICE	
NOTES:					

DATE		ORDER	
RETURN CUSTOMER	YES	NO	....

CUSTOMER DETAILS

NAME		SHIPPING ADRESS	
TEL			
EMAIL			
COMPANY		DATE SHIPPED	TRACKING No.
SHIPPING METHOD			

ITEM NO.	ITEM DESCRIPTION	QTY.	PRICE	DISCOUNT	TAX	TOTAL PRICE

COMFIRMATON

TOTAL UNIT PRICE		ADVANCED PAID		PAYMENT METHOD	
TOTAL DISCOUNT		REMAINING PAID		DATE PAID	
TOTAL TAX		TOTAL QUANTITY		FINAL PRICE	
NOTES:					

DATE			ORDER
RETURN CUSTOMER	YES	NO	

CUSTOMER DETAILS

NAME		SHIPPING ADRESS	
TEL			
EMAIL			
COMPANY		DATE SHIPPED	TRACKING No.
SHIPPING METHOD			

ITEM NO.	ITEM DESCRIPTION	QTY.	PRICE	DISCOUNT	TAX	TOTAL PRICE

COMFIRMATON

TOTAL UNIT PRICE		ADVANCED PAID		PAYMENT METHOD	
TOTAL DISCOUNT		REMAINING PAID		DATE PAID	
TOTAL TAX		TOTAL QUANTITY		FINAL PRICE	
NOTES:					

DATE		ORDER	
RETURN CUSTOMER	YES	NO	

CUSTOMER DETAILS

NAME		SHIPPING ADRESS	
TEL			
EMAIL			
COMPANY		DATE SHIPPED	TRACKING No.
SHIPPING METHOD			

ITEM NO.	ITEM DESCRIPTION	QTY.	PRICE	DISCOUNT	TAX	TOTAL PRICE

COMFIRMATON

TOTAL UNIT PRICE		ADVANCED PAID		PAYMENT METHOD	
TOTAL DISCOUNT		REMAINING PAID		DATE PAID	
TOTAL TAX		TOTAL QUANTITY		FINAL PRICE	

NOTES:

Return and Exchange Form

FROM		REPORT DATE:
		REPORT ISSUE:
SHIP TO:		DATE OF REPORT/ EXCHANGE:

ITEM	DESCRIPTION	QTY	UNIT PRICE	TOTAL AMOUNT

	CREDIT ISSUE
DATE SHIPPED	
CUSTOMER ORDER #	
OUR ORDER #	

NOTES

Return and Exchange Form

FROM		REPORT DATE:
		REPORT ISSUE:
SHIP TO:		DATE OF REPORT/ EXCHANGE:

ITEM	DESCRIPTION	QTY	UNIT PRICE	TOTAL AMOUNT

	CREDIT ISSUE
DATE SHIPPED	
CUSTOMER ORDER #	
OUR ORDER #	

NOTES

Return and Exchange Form

FROM		REPORT DATE:
		REPORT ISSUE:
SHIP TO:		DATE OF REPORT/ EXCHANGE:

ITEM	DESCRIPTION	QTY	UNIT PRICE	TOTAL AMOUNT

DATE SHIPPED	CREDIT ISSUE
CUSTOMER ORDER #	
OUR ORDER #	

NOTES

Return and Exchange Form

FROM	REPORT DATE:
	REPORT ISSUE:
SHIP TO:	DATE OF REPORT/ EXCHANGE:

ITEM	DESCRIPTION	QTY	UNIT PRICE	TOTAL AMOUNT

DATE SHIPPED	CREDIT ISSUE
CUSTOMER ORDER #	
OUR ORDER #	

NOTES

Return and Exchange Form

FROM	REPORT DATE:
	REPORT ISSUE:
SHIP TO:	DATE OF REPORT/ EXCHANGE:

ITEM	DESCRIPTION	QTY	UNIT PRICE	TOTAL AMOUNT

	CREDIT ISSUE
DATE SHIPPED	
CUSTOMER ORDER #	
OUR ORDER #	

NOTES

Return and Exchange Form

FROM	**REPORT DATE:**
	REPORT ISSUE:
SHIP TO:	**DATE OF REPORT/ EXCHANGE:**

ITEM	DESCRIPTION	QTY	UNIT PRICE	TOTAL AMOUNT

DATE SHIPPED	**CREDIT ISSUE**
CUSTOMER ORDER #	
OUR ORDER #	

NOTES

Monthly Budget Planner

MONTH		YEAR	
SPENDING BUDGET GOAL		INCOME GOAL	

INCOME BREAKDOWN

DATE	DESCRIPTION	AMOUNT

FIXED EXPENSES			VARIABLE EXPENSES		
DATE	DESCRIPTION	AMOUNT	DATE	DESCRIPTION	AMOUNT

	BUDGETED	ACTUAL	DIFFERENCE
TOTAL INCOME			
TOTAL EXPENSES			

Monthly Budget Planner

MONTH		YEAR	
SPENDING BUDGET GOAL		INCOME GOAL	

INCOME BREAKDOWN

DATE	DESCRIPTION	AMOUNT

FIXED EXPENSES				VARIABLE EXPENSES		
DATE	DESCRIPTION	AMOUNT		DATE	DESCRIPTION	AMOUNT

	BUDGETED	ACTUAL	DIFFERENCE
TOTAL INCOME			
TOTAL EXPENSES			

Monthly Budget Planner

MONTH		YEAR	
SPENDING BUDGET GOAL		**INCOME GOAL**	

INCOME BREAKDOWN

DATE	DESCRIPTION	AMOUNT

FIXED EXPENSES

DATE	DESCRIPTION	AMOUNT

VARIABLE EXPENSES

DATE	DESCRIPTION	AMOUNT

	BUDGETED	ACTUAL	DIFFERENCE
TOTAL INCOME			
TOTAL EXPENSES			

Monthly Budget Planner

MONTH		YEAR	
SPENDING BUDGET GOAL		INCOME GOAL	

INCOME BREAKDOWN

DATE	DESCRIPTION	AMOUNT

FIXED EXPENSES

DATE	DESCRIPTION	AMOUNT

VARIABLE EXPENSES

DATE	DESCRIPTION	AMOUNT

	BUDGETED	ACTUAL	DIFFERENCE
TOTAL INCOME			
TOTAL EXPENSES			

Monthly Budget Planner

MONTH		YEAR	
SPENDING BUDGET GOAL		**INCOME GOAL**	

INCOME BREAKDOWN

DATE	DESCRIPTION	AMOUNT

FIXED EXPENSES

DATE	DESCRIPTION	AMOUNT

VARIABLE EXPENSES

DATE	DESCRIPTION	AMOUNT

	BUDGETED	ACTUAL	DIFFERENCE
TOTAL INCOME			
TOTAL EXPENSES			

Monthly Budget Planner

MONTH		YEAR	
SPENDING BUDGET GOAL		INCOME GOAL	

INCOME BREAKDOWN

DATE	DESCRIPTION	AMOUNT

FIXED EXPENSES

DATE	DESCRIPTION	AMOUNT

VARIABLE EXPENSES

DATE	DESCRIPTION	AMOUNT

	BUDGETED	ACTUAL	DIFFERENCE
TOTAL INCOME			
TOTAL EXPENSES			

Monthly Budget Planner

MONTH		YEAR	
SPENDING BUDGET GOAL		INCOME GOAL	

INCOME BREAKDOWN

DATE	DESCRIPTION	AMOUNT

FIXED EXPENSES				VARIABLE EXPENSES		
DATE	DESCRIPTION	AMOUNT		DATE	DESCRIPTION	AMOUNT

	BUDGETED	ACTUAL	DIFFERENCE
TOTAL INCOME			
TOTAL EXPENSES			

Monthly Budget Planner

MONTH		YEAR	
SPENDING BUDGET GOAL		**INCOME GOAL**	

INCOME BREAKDOWN

DATE	DESCRIPTION	AMOUNT

FIXED EXPENSES

DATE	DESCRIPTION	AMOUNT

VARIABLE EXPENSES

DATE	DESCRIPTION	AMOUNT

	BUDGETED	ACTUAL	DIFFERENCE
TOTAL INCOME			
TOTAL EXPENSES			

Monthly Budget Planner

MONTH		YEAR	
SPENDING BUDGET GOAL		INCOME GOAL	

INCOME BREAKDOWN

DATE	DESCRIPTION	AMOUNT

FIXED EXPENSES

DATE	DESCRIPTION	AMOUNT

VARIABLE EXPENSES

DATE	DESCRIPTION	AMOUNT

	BUDGETED	ACTUAL	DIFFERENCE
TOTAL INCOME			
TOTAL EXPENSES			

Monthly Budget Planner

MONTH		YEAR	
SPENDING BUDGET GOAL		**INCOME GOAL**	

INCOME BREAKDOWN

DATE	DESCRIPTION	AMOUNT

FIXED EXPENSES

DATE	DESCRIPTION	AMOUNT

VARIABLE EXPENSES

DATE	DESCRIPTION	AMOUNT

	BUDGETED	ACTUAL	DIFFERENCE
TOTAL INCOME			
TOTAL EXPENSES			

Monthly Budget Planner

MONTH		YEAR	
SPENDING BUDGET GOAL		**INCOME GOAL**	

INCOME BREAKDOWN

DATE	DESCRIPTION	AMOUNT

FIXED EXPENSES

DATE	DESCRIPTION	AMOUNT

VARIABLE EXPENSES

DATE	DESCRIPTION	AMOUNT

	BUDGETED	ACTUAL	DIFFERENCE
TOTAL INCOME			
TOTAL EXPENSES			

Monthly Budget Planner

MONTH		YEAR	
SPENDING BUDGET GOAL		**INCOME GOAL**	

INCOME BREAKDOWN

DATE	DESCRIPTION	AMOUNT

FIXED EXPENSES				VARIABLE EXPENSES		
DATE	DESCRIPTION	AMOUNT		DATE	DESCRIPTION	AMOUNT

	BUDGETED	ACTUAL	DIFFERENCE
TOTAL INCOME			
TOTAL EXPENSES			

Monthly Sales Tracker

Month _____

DATE	CATEGORY	DISCRIPTION	AMOUNT	BALANCE

Monthly Sales Tracker

Month _____

DATE	CATEGORY	DISCRIPTION	AMOUNT	BALANCE

Monthly Sales Tracker

Month _____

DATE	CATEGORY	DISCRIPTION	AMOUNT	BALANCE
DATE	CATEGORY	DISCRIPTION	AMOUNT	BALANCE

Monthly Sales Tracker

Month _____

DATE	CATEGORY	DISCRIPTION	AMOUNT	BALANCE

Monthly Sales Tracker

Month _____

DATE	CATEGORY	DISCRIPTION	AMOUNT	BALANCE

Monthly Sales Tracker

Month _____

DATE	CATEGORY	DISCRIPTION	AMOUNT	BALANCE

Monthly Sales Tracker

Month _____

DATE	CATEGORY	DISCRIPTION	AMOUNT	BALANCE

Monthly Sales Tracker

Month _____

DATE	CATEGORY	DISCRIPTION	AMOUNT	BALANCE

Monthly Sales Tracker

Month _____

DATE	CATEGORY	DISCRIPTION	AMOUNT	BALANCE

Monthly Sales Tracker

Month _____

DATE	CATEGORY	DISCRIPTION	AMOUNT	BALANCE

Monthly Sales Tracker

Month _____

DATE	CATEGORY	DISCRIPTION	AMOUNT	BALANCE

Monthly Sales Tracker

Month _____

DATE	CATEGORY	DISCRIPTION	AMOUNT	BALANCE

RETURN TRACKER

DATE	ORDER	CUSTOMER	ITEMS	QTY.	PRICE	RECEIVED

RETURN TRACKER

DATE	ORDER	CUSTOMER	ITEMS	QTY.	PRICE	RECEIVED

Annual Profits

	INCOME	SUPPLY COST	SHIPPING	FEES	OTHER EXPENSES	PROFIT
JAN						
FEB						
MAR						
APR						
MAY						
JUN						
JUL						
AUG						
SEP						
OCT						
NOV						
DEC						

www.ingramcontent.com/pod-product-compliance
Lightning Source LLC
Chambersburg PA
CBHW081519220526
45467CB00010B/2976